BODY SYSTEMS

Breathing

Jackie Hardie

RIGBY
INTERACTIVE
LIBRARY

Interiors designed by Inklines and Small House Design
Illustrations by Catherine Ward, except:
Peter Bull Art Studio, p. 4 (left) and pp. 22–23;
Garden Studio/Darren Patterson, p. 27.

Printed in the United Kingdom

00 99 98 97 96
10 9 8 7 6 5 4 3 2 1

Library of Congress Cataloging-in-Publication Data
Hardie, Jackie, 1944 –
  Breathing and respiration / Jackie Hardie.
    p. cm. – (Body systems)
Includes bibliographical references and index.
Summary: Describes the different parts of the body's breathing
system, how they work, and how they are affected by pollution, smoking, and asthma.
    ISBN 1-57572-096-5 (library)
    1. Respiration – Juvenile literature 2. Respiratory organs – Juvenile literature.
[1. Respiratory system. 2. Respiration.] I. Title. II. Series: Body systems (Crystal Lake, Ill.)
QP121.H336 1997
612.2–dc20

                                                        96-30164
                                                           CIP
                                                           AC

Acknowledgments
The publisher would like to thank the following for permission to reproduce
photographs: Action-Plus Photographic, p. 5, p. 14, p. 28; Allsport USA, p. 13; Hulton Deutsch
Collection, p. 27; NHPA/Martin Harvey, p. 25; Oxford Scientific Films, p. 10;
Science Photo Library, p. 3, p. 7 (both), p. 8, p. 9, p. 19, p. 20, p. 21, p. 23 (both), p. 29;
Tony Stone Images, p. 4, p. 24; Zefa, p. 17.

Every effort has been made to contact copyright holders of any material reproduced in this book.
Any omissions will be rectified in subsequent printings if notice is given to the publisher.

Note to the Reader
Some words in this book are printed in **bold** type. This indicates that the word is listed in the
glossary on pages 30–31. This glossary gives a brief explanation of words that may be new to you.

Visit Rigby's Education Station® on the World Wide Web at http://www.rigby.com

Contents

Why You Need to Breathe

L ike most people, you probably take the workings of your body for granted. You digest your food. Your heart beats regularly. You breathe air in and out without even thinking about it. You have been breathing ever since you were born, in fact—but why? What does breathing do for you? Here's the answer: it brings **oxygen** into your body and pushes out **carbon dioxide.**

Giving you energy

Your body **cells** need energy to stay alive. They get this energy from food. They must have oxygen to burn the food to release the energy—a process called **respiration.** Oxygen is found in air, and that is why you breathe in air. As your cells burn food, carbon dioxide and water form. Your cells cannot use these substances, so you breathe out to get rid of them.

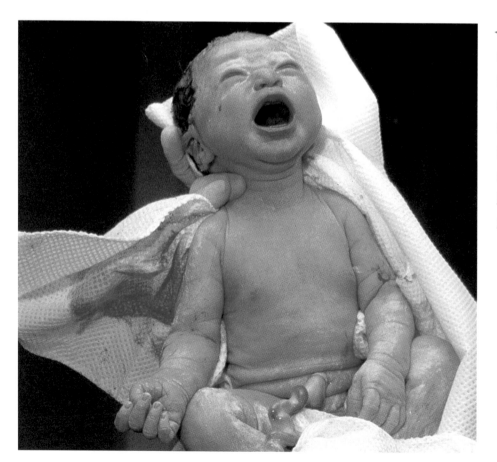

◄ A baby takes her first breath. Before she was born, the baby received the oxygen she needed from her mother's blood.

The breathing organ

In very small, thin animals, such as flatworms, all the body cells are near the surface. Oxygen can get directly to their cells by moving through their body surfaces. Bigger animals, however, need a special system to get oxygen to all their cells. It is called the respiratory system. This system brings air or water into special breathing organs. (Most air-breathing animals, for example, have **lungs.** Fish have **gills.**) These **breathing organs** have many thin, flat, moist parts inside them. Oxygen moves through the moist surfaces into the blood. Carbon dioxide moves out of the blood through the moist surfaces and into the air or water. The blood with oxygen goes to the cells. The air or water with carbon dioxide leaves the body.

▲ *This water beetle breathes under water from a bubble of air it has collected.*

Did you know?

Some insects breathe in air even though they live in water. They capture air in a bubble and then position the bubble near the openings to their breathing system. The insect gets its oxygen from the air in the bubble.

Your Breathing System

Your **breathing system** runs from your nose and mouth to your lungs. Air enters your body through your nose or mouth. It moves through your **windpipe** and **bronchi** to your lungs. There, the tubes divide into even smaller branches that end in tiny bags. Oxygen moves through the thin walls of these bags into your blood. Red cells in your blood stream carry the oxygen to your cells. The remaining air meanwhile, picks up carbon dioxide and water vapor and leaves your body.

Taking a deep breath

Your lungs are in your chest. This area is separated from your lower body by the **diaphragm.** Your chest moves when you breathe because your ribs and diaphragm are moving. Muscles in your chest pull your diaphragm down and your ribs up. This opens up your lungs, which makes air rush into them. When the muscles let go, your **rib cage** closes and the air is squeezed again. That is how you breathe in and out.

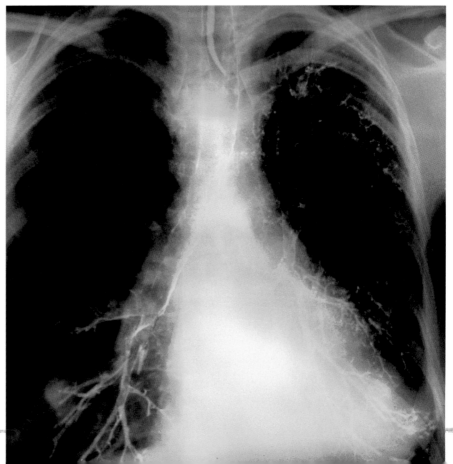

▶ *X-ray photograph of a person's chest, showing the windpipe dividing into two tubes (the* bronchi*) and then into smaller and smaller tubes* **(bronchioles)** *inside the lung on the left.*

Taking oxygen to your cells

Blood collects oxygen and carries it to the cells. The cells use the oxygen to burn food and thus create energy. Carbon dioxide is made when the energy is used.

Blood collects waste carbon dioxide from the cells in your body and takes it to the lungs. Here the unwanted gas is breathed out, and the cycle starts again. In fact, it never stops.

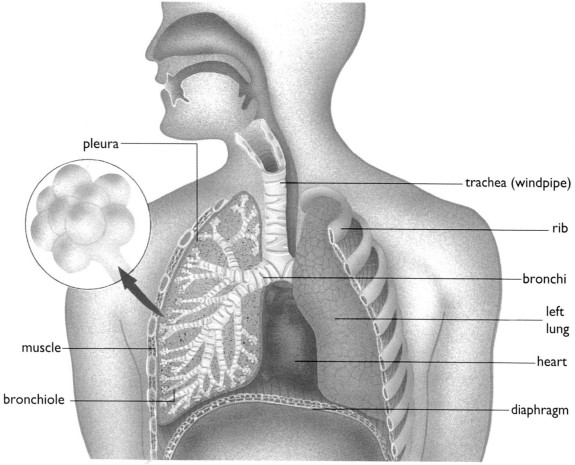

pleura

trachea (windpipe)

rib

bronchi

left lung

muscle

heart

bronchiole

diaphragm

▲ *The respiratory system, from the mouth and nose to the two lungs inside the chest.*

Did you know?
Breathing usually runs on 'automatic pilot'—you don't think about it. This is just as well when you are sleeping! You can control your breathing up to a point, which is useful for activities like swimming.

Inside Your Head

When you breathe in air through your nostrils, your nose does several useful jobs. It warms the incoming air, filters out the dust, and helps deal with the germs that you draw in with every breath.

Inside your nose

Your nose has two nostrils. Each nostril leads into a space called a **nasal cavity.** This space forms an airway that leads to your throat and then to your windpipe or **trachea.** The nasal cavity is lined with a layer of cells that are well supplied with blood. Some of the cells in the lining make a slimy fluid called **mucus.** These cells have fine hairs, called **cilia,** which beat all the time.

This movement pushes a layer of mucus along like a stream, carrying dirt and dust with it. The mucus is pushed towards the nostrils, where you get rid of it when you blow your nose or sneeze. Cilia in the breathing tubes in your chest push the mucus towards the top of the windpipe and you then swallow it. Any germs in the mucus are killed by the acid in your stomach.

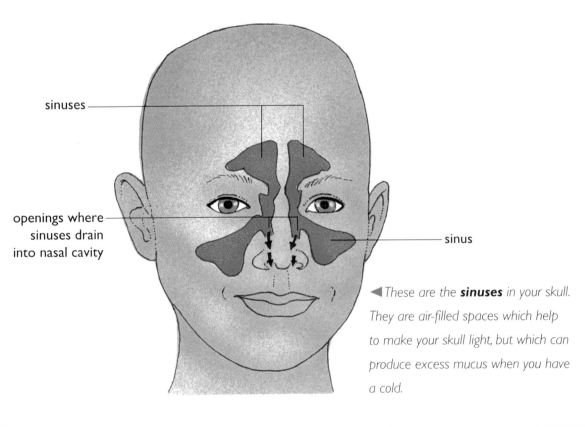

sinuses

openings where sinuses drain into nasal cavity

sinus

*◀ These are the **sinuses** in your skull. They are air-filled spaces which help to make your skull light, but which can produce excess mucus when you have a cold.*

Having a cold

If your skull were made of solid bone it would be much heavier and you would have to work harder to hold it up. But the bones near your nasal cavity have hollow spaces called sinuses. These help make your skull light. But when you have a cold, the lining of these cavities may swell and make lots of mucus, which gives you a runny nose and a headache.

Swallowing

When you swallow, the **soft palate** blocks the airway from the nasal cavity. A small flap (the epiglottis) covers the opening of the windpipe. This stops food from going down the windpipe, which would choke you. Instead, food goes down the **esophagus** (gullet) to the stomach. If food lands on the epiglottis, you cough and splutter until it goes down the right way.

▶ *When your mouth is wide open, you can see the **uvula** hanging down above the throat.*

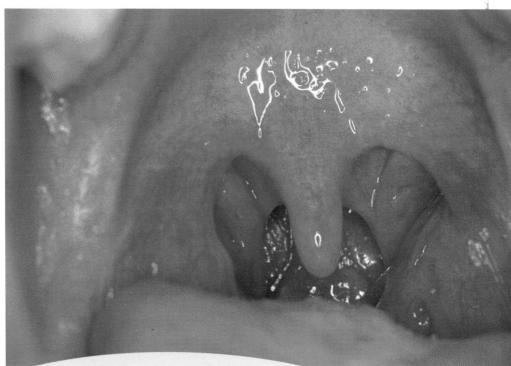

Did you know?

No one knows for sure what the uvula at the back of your mouth is for. It is part of the soft palate and it may be there to make sure there is a good seal as the air passages are shut off when you swallow. One thing is known for sure: the uvula has nothing to do with the voice. So when you see cartoon characters with a flap that is wobbling in a frenzy, the cartoonist has got it wrong!

Inside Your Chest

Your ribs, backbone, and chest bone (sternum) make a cage around your lungs, protecting them from harm. The floor of the cage is the diaphragm. During breathing, muscles stretch the rib cage open and pull the diaphragm down, then let go. These movements stretch the lungs open, filling them with air, and then squash them, squeezing the air out.

Into your lungs

When you breathe in, air goes down your windpipe, or trachea. This tube divides into two branches called the bronchial tubes. Each bronchial tube goes into one of your two lungs, then branches off many times to form bronchioles.

The walls of the windpipe and bronchial tubes are strengthened by rings of **cartilage.** The rings of cartilage hold them open and allow the air to flow through freely, just like the ridges on the hose of a vacuum cleaner.

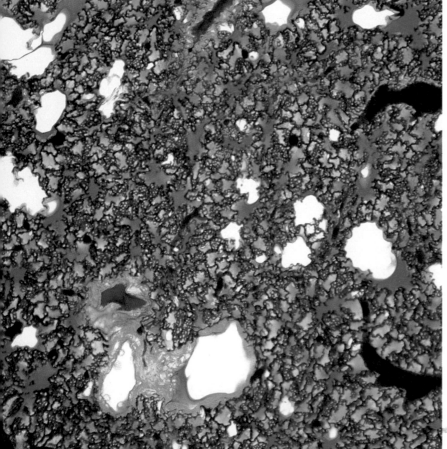

◀ *If all the* **air sacs (alveoli)** *in a person's lungs could be laid flat, the total surface area for breathing would be the size of a tennis court.*

Into your blood

At the tips of the finest bronchioles are the air sacs, or **alveoli.** They look like tiny clusters of balloons, or grapes on a vine. The walls of each alveolus are very thin—in fact only two cells thick. Each alveolus has a lot of very fine blood vessels **(capillaries)** around it. Gases inside the alveolus can move quickly and easily through its walls into the blood in the blood vessels. Gases from the blood can move just as easily back into the alveolus.

There are about 300 million tiny air sacs filling your two lungs. If you could open the air sacs and lay them flat, they would make a carpet about 39 feet long and 26 feet wide, which is about the size of a tennis court. Together, these sacs, the tubes, and the blood vessels make up the spongy lungs.

blood from network of capillaries

blood to network of capillaries

thin wall of the alveoli

▲ Air sacs or alveoli, with their blood supply, at the tip of a bronchiole. There are about 300 million of these in your lungs.

Did you know?

When you breathe in and out, you move air at about 5 miles an hour. But when you sneeze, the air speed is more like 100 miles an hour! A single sneeze can shoot 20,000 drops of moisture into the air up to about 13 feet away. So, if you have a cold, use a handkerchief to avoid infecting other people.

Breathing Movements

When sitting still, you breathe about 15 to 18 times a minute. You can change how quickly or how deeply you breathe for a short time, but as soon as you stop thinking about it, your breathing goes back to normal. Each breath is about 500 cubic cm of air (about as much air as milk in a small carton). If you run, you take deeper breaths, and more of them. This brings more oxygen into your blood to help produce the extra energy you need.

Moving your chest

When you breathe, your chest changes shape as muscles move your ribs and diaphragm. When you **inhale,** or breathe in, the diaphragm is pulled down and your rib cage moves up. This makes the space inside your chest bigger. Air rushes in to fill the space. In **exhaling,** or breathing out, the diaphragm moves up and the rib cage is lowered. The space inside your chest gets smaller and you breathe out. Air is forced out of the lungs.

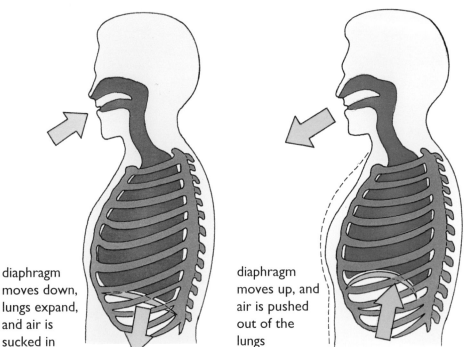

◄ The changes inside your chest as you breathe in and out.

diaphragm moves down, lungs expand, and air is sucked in

diaphragm moves up, and air is pushed out of the lungs

Pleural layers

The lungs are surrounded by a tough double layer, called the **pleura.** In the space between the layers, there is a slippery fluid. The outer pleura lines the rib cage and diaphragm.

The inner pluera forms a layer on the lungs. These pleural layers and the fluid between them help to make breathing movements smooth and keep the ribs from damaging the lungs.

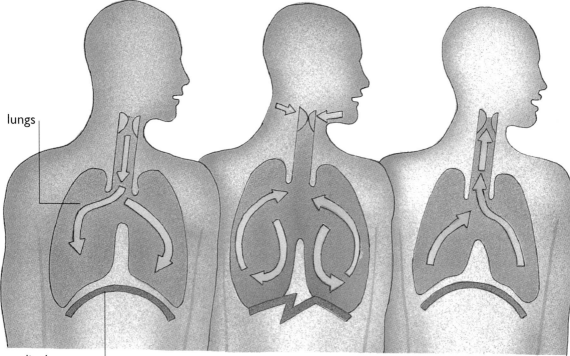

lungs

diaphragm

1. Normal breath comes in.

2. Diaphragm twitches, top of windpipe snaps shut.

3. Normal breath goes out.

▲ Twitch of the diaphragm during hiccups.

Hiccups

If you get hiccups, it is because your diaphragm is twitching. This happens if you eat too much, eat spicy foods, or swallow foods that are too hot or too cold. There are many cures, and you have to find one that works for you. Some people breathe the same air in and out into a paper bag. Others hold their breath.

Did you know?

When you get a stitch, you have a cramp in your diaphragm. If you bend over and touch your toes, you usually stretch your diaphragm enough to relieve the cramp.

What Happens to the Air You Breathe?

Air is a mixture of gases including oxygen, **nitrogen,** and a small amount of water vapor and carbon dioxide. Air that is breathed in and air that is breathed out contain different amounts of these gases. Breathing removes some oxygen and adds carbon dioxide and water vapor. If you breathe out onto a cold window or mirror, the water vapor you breathe out will condense and change into liquid water, making the glass "steam up."

Release of energy

Every living cell in your body uses oxygen to burn sugar from the food you eat. This process releases energy, which keeps the cells, and thus your body, working. Sugar and oxygen are used up inside the cells. Two waste substances, carbon dioxide and water vapor, are made. Some of the water may be used by the cells, but some is breathed out, along with the carbon dioxide. These chemical changes are the reason that the air you exhale is different from the air you breathe in.

◀ *The water vapor in the air you breathe out will form drops of water on cool surfaces.*

Moving gases around the body

Burning food to release energy uses oxygen and makes carbon dioxide. The blood is what moves these gases around the body. Red blood cells carry the oxygen, and this **oxygenated blood** is bright red. The red blood cells then pass close to cells that need oxygen.

The oxygen leaves the blood, and carbon dioxide enters it. The resulting **deoxygenated blood** is a dull red. Back in the lungs, the carbon dioxide passes from the blood and into the air sacs or alveoli, and it is then breathed out.

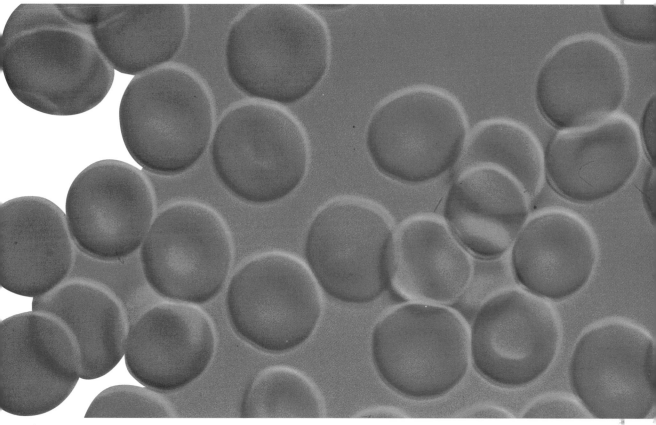

▲ Red blood cells.

Did you know?

Tourists have been banned from visiting some sites where there are prehistoric cave paintings. They have also been stopped from visiting the inside of some of the pyramids in Egypt. This is because over the years the breathed-out air of many tourists— and the carbon dioxide it contains—has damaged the paintings or the stone.

Pollution

Our breathing system works best with air that is clean. But today, the air often contains harmful gases such as **sulfur dioxide** and **carbon monoxide.** These gases come mainly from factories, automobiles, and cigarette smoke. Harmful waste products such as these, which can damage our natural and everyday surroundings, are called **pollution.**

Air pollution

Burning fossil fuels such as coal, oil, and natural gas, produce sulfur dioxide and carbon monoxide. Sulfur dioxide dissolves in water and forms an acid. So when the gas is breathed in, it may irritate the moist linings of breathing passages and cause a runny nose. The breathing tubes and air sacs in the lungs may also be damaged by this acid, which makes lung diseases more likely. When sulfur dioxide dissolves in rainwater, it may be carried away from the place it was made. In this way the pollution may spread. The polluted rainwater is called acid rain.

◄ *Smoke from factory chimneys can cause damage to health.*

Car exhausts

Burning fuels, such as gasoline, produce carbon monoxide. If this gas reaches a **red blood cell,** it stops the cell from carrying oxygen. So, to carry enough oxygen, the body needs to make new red cells. If there is a lot of carbon monoxide, people can't make enough red cells. They have to breathe faster to get the oxygen they need.

In the recent past smoke belched from car exhausts often contained lead. This came from a substance added to gasoline to make car engines run more smoothly. In the 1980s it was found that children living near major highways had high levels of lead in their blood. Lead in the blood can interfere with the development of the brain. Today, only unleaded gasoline may be sold in U.S. gas stations—it's the law.

▲ The fumes in car exhausts may contain many dangerous chemicals such as carbon monoxide, ozone, unburned hydrocarbons, lead, and oxides of nitrogen.

Did you know?

Many industries produce chemicals that pollute the air. This may damage the lungs of workers in the industry and of people who live nearby. Miners are likely to suffer from a disease called pneumoconiosis. Workers in asbestos factories may suffer from asbestosis, where the fibers from asbestos become embedded in the lungs.

▲ This worker is wearing a mask, which screens out the impurities from the air he is breathing.

Smoking

Cigarettes are made from the dried, shredded leaves of the tobacco plant. The habit of inhaling smoke for pleasure started hundreds of years ago, probably in South America. The smoke from burning tobacco contains dozens of chemicals. The main drug in cigarette smoking is **nicotine.** Most people who smoke become **addicted** to nicotine, making it harder for them to give up the habit of smoking.

Damage from nicotine

Nicotine and **tar** breathed in with cigarette smoke may eventually stop the cleaning cells in the breathing tubes from working. Nicotine that enters the blood of a smoker through the lungs may affect the nervous system. Tar, a sticky brown substance, collects deep in the lungs. This may lead to **lung cancer** and other illnesses. Smokers have a high risk of other serious diseases later in life as well.

People who smoke die, on average, at a younger age than people who don't smoke. For instance, a 25-year-old man who smokes 40 cigarettes a day can expect to live 8.3 years fewer than one who does not smoke. You don't even have to light up yourself. If you spend time with smokers, you breathe in the smoke from their cigarettes. This **passive smoking** can seriously damage your health.

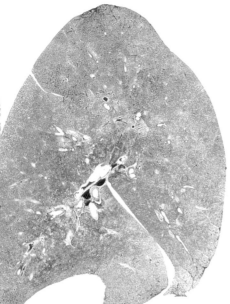

◄ ►Tar deposits in one of these thin slices of two human lungs show clearly which lung belonged to a smoker and which to a nonsmoker.

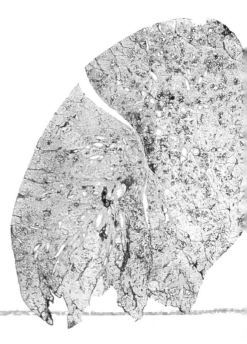

This table reserved for smokers.

WANT TO STOP? PHONE THE SMOKELINE ON 0800 84 84 84. YOU CAN DO IT. WE CAN HELP.

▲ Governments in many countries advertise the dangers of smoking with posters like this one.

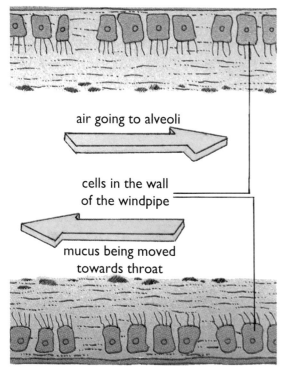

air going to alveoli

cells in the wall of the windpipe

mucus being moved towards throat

▲ In the windpipe, dust and dirt are trapped in sticky mucus. The cilia beat to move the dirty mucus away from the lungs.

Did you know?
About 400,000 people in the United States die each year from illnesses related to smoking.

Breathlessness

Smokers get out of breath easily. They also produce a lot of mucus, and they have to cough to remove it. This can lead to **bronchitis.** Carbon monoxide from smoke gets into the red blood cells and stops them from carrying oxygen. The smoker has to breathe faster to get enough oxygen and this can strain the heart.

Pregnancy

Many substances in the mother's blood pass into her baby's blood in her **womb.** These include alcohol and the chemicals from cigarette smoke. Pregnant women who smoke are more likely to lose the baby before it is fully developed. Their babies are also more likely to die in the first week after birth.

Asthma

In the western world, about 3 people out of 100 suffer from **asthma.** Asthma is more common in people who live in the city than among those who live in the countryside. Sometimes asthma is triggered by **allergens** in the surroundings, such as car exhaust fumes, **house dust mites** or **pollen** grains. For some people, even laughing, frying food, or smelling paint may start an asthma attack.

What is asthma?

"Asthma" means "to breathe hard." If you have asthma, you may suddenly find yourself short of breath and wheezing, especially when you breathe out. Your chest feels tight, and you may get a cough. The attack then passes, and your breathing returns to normal.

During an attack, three things happen in your lungs at the same time. The muscles in the walls of the breathing tubes contract, more mucus is made there, and the inside walls of the tubes swell. If treated quickly, all three things can be put back to normal.

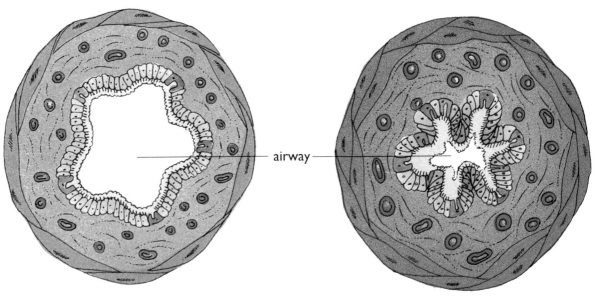

normal

during an attack

airway

▲ *This is what happens during an asthma attack. A slice through a bronchiole shows how the airway becomes narrow and makes breathing difficult.*

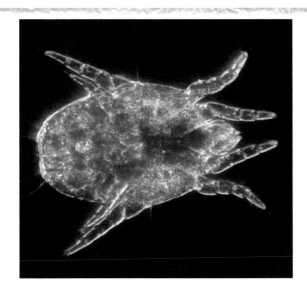

▲ A house dust mite, much magnified. Many people believe mites in carpets, mattresses, and household dust trigger asthma attacks.

Treating asthma

During an attack an asthma sufferer may need an **inhaler.** This contains a drug which opens up (dilates) the breathing tubes, so the drug is known as a bronchodilator. If you use an inhaler, it is important to take in a deep breath at the same time as you press down the top of the inhaler. This helps to get the spray of the drug into the lungs where it is needed.

▲ This girl is using an inhaler to spray a broncho-dilator drug into her lungs. This helps to widen the breathing tubes.

Did you know?

Many people have asthma, but with the right treatment they can still lead active and successful lives. President Theodore Roosevelt had asthma. So does basketball star Sam Perkins. So do U.S. track stars Jackie Joyner-Kersee and Florence Griffiths-Joyner, both Olympic gold medal winners.

Breathing in Unusual Places

Astronauts and deep-sea divers work where there is no air. They must be given a special supply of air to stay alive. Usually, the air is supplied from cylinders.

Breathing under water

The first aqualung or scuba (*s*elf *c*ontained *u*nderwater *b*reathing *a*pparatus) was invented in 1942 by the French marine biologist Jacques Cousteau. When a diver dives to a great depth below the surface, water presses heavily on his or her chest, which makes it harder to breathe. The aqualung helps the diver by supplying air at high pressure.

At this high pressure, the nitrogen as well as the oxygen in the air dissolves in the diver's blood. This doesn't cause any harm while the diver is deep down. But if he or she comes up too quickly, the nitrogen comes out of the blood as air bubbles, a condition called "the bends." The diver will die if bubbles form in the fine blood vessels of the brain and heart.

◄ People working underwater need a supply of air. They wear aqualungs.

Breathing in high places

In the high mountains the amount of oxygen in the air is less than at sea level. When people arrive by air at cities high above sea level, they find it hard to breathe at first. They may get out of breath even when sleeping. However, they get used to the air if they live in such a place for a week or two. This is called getting acclimatized. Their bodies have made more red blood cells. Their blood can now carry enough oxygen to supply all their body cells.

Did you know?

If you could count the number of red blood cells in a drop of blood about the size of this spot (•), you would find five million of them. Five million! People who live at high altitudes have more than seven million!

Some athletes train at high altitudes, so their bodies make more red blood cells and their blood can carry more oxygen. These athletes believe that when they return to places nearer sea level, they will be able to perform better in their events than athletes who have not trained in this way.

Champion distance runners from countries such as Kenya and Ethiopia may owe some of their success to the fact that they grew up in places high above sea level.

◄ *Moses Kiptanui of Kenya wins the steeplechase at the 1995 World Championships in Gothenburg, Sweden.*

Your Voice

Wen you speak, the sounds you make come from the **voice box,** or **larynx,** at the top of your windpipe. Sounds are made when air passes over your **vocal cords.** You shape these sounds into recognizable words with your lips, teeth, and tongue.

In the voice box

You can feel your voice box, or larynx, at the front of your neck. It is at the top end of your windpipe. The sides of the larynx are kept rigid by cartilage. The inner lining of the voice box has two pairs of folds. The upper pair forms a valve that allows you to hold your breath.

The lower pair, the vocal cords, stretch across the opening from the front to the back. The vocal cords are two flat white bands. They are about .5 to .7 of an inch long in women, .7 to one inch long in men. Most of the time your vocal cords are kept apart. Air flows freely through the V-shaped opening between them, and no sound is made.

▶ *The voice box is at the top of the windpipe, and it contains the vocal cords.*

windpipe

voice box

esophagus (food pipe)

Making the sounds

When the vocal cords are stretched and air from your lungs is forced between them, the cords tremble, or vibrate, and a sound is made. If the vocal cords are stretched tight and are close together, the sound is high **pitched:** the cords vibrate many times per second.

When the vocal cords are looser and further apart, the sound is low pitched. The range of a particular person's voice—the difference between its highest and lowest pitched sounds that the voice produces— depends on the thickness and length of their vocal cords.

▲ *This girl can feel her vocal cords vibrate when she says something.*

Did you know?

The number of vibrations of the vocal cords ranges from about 80 per second in a man talking in a deep voice to about 1,400 per second in a woman singing in a very high-pitched tone. The number of vibrations is called the **frequency***.*

Turning Sounds into Words

Most mammals—humans, dogs, cattle, and mice for example—have a voice box. But only humans produce the great variety of sounds known as **speech.** People combine sounds in different ways to form the words of a **language.**

Forming words

When you speak, air passes between your vocal cords and goes on up to the space behind your tongue, into your mouth, and past the lips. Movements of your lips, and of the tongue against your teeth and the roof of your mouth (palate), shape the sound into words.

Most of the words you speak are a combination of vowel and consonant sounds. When you make an "f" sound, your top teeth are over your lower lip as you force air through. If you put your tongue under your top teeth and blow through your lips you will get a "th" sound. In an "m" or an "n" sound, the air in the nasal cavity vibrates.

Intonation

In some languages a rise or fall in the pitch of the voice gives a meaning to a whole sentence. For example, it can show whether a sentence is a question or a statement. In other languages, such as Cantonese Chinese, **intonation** gives meaning to single words. The same set of sounds can have three different meanings, depending on whether it is said with a rising, falling, or level pitch.

▶ *Parts of the mouth that are important in producing speech.*

nasal cavity

lips

teeth

epiglottis

voice box

palate

tongue

windpipe

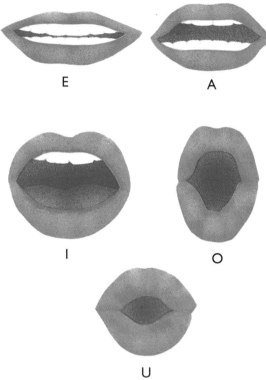

E A

I O

U

▲ *The lips form a different shape for each vowel sound.*

Did you know?

The Khoisan languages of southern Africa use clicks and other types of "stop" made in the throat or nose. One such language has 48 different click sounds.

Unfamiliar sounds

Some speech sounds do not use the air stream from the lungs. One of the most common is the "click," a sharp sound made by the tongue or lips. You probably use a click sound to show disapproval. In some languages, in southern Africa for example, clicks are used as consonants. Clicks are very common in these languages, making them sound strange to people who are unfamiliar with languages of this type.

▶ *Singer Miriam Makeba uses click sounds in the songs she sings from southern Africa.*

Artificial Breathing

When people drown or **suffocate,** they stop breathing. They may stop breathing during an **epileptic seizure,** too. This is called **asphyxia.** When it happens, it is important to get oxygen into the victim's blood quickly. More than four minutes without oxygen can cause brain damage or death. If you know what to do in such an emergency, you might save somebody's life.

Artificial resuscitation

Starting the breathing again is called **artificial resuscitation.** All emergency workers are trained to do it. The worker checks that the mouth and throat are clear. Then he or she breathes out, blowing air into the victim's mouth or nose. This air contains oxygen.

If the emergency worker is blowing into the mouth, the victim's nose must be held closed, but if he or she is blowing into the nose, the mouth must be closed. Either way, it is important to tilt the victim's head well back, so that the victim's tongue does not block his or her windpipe.

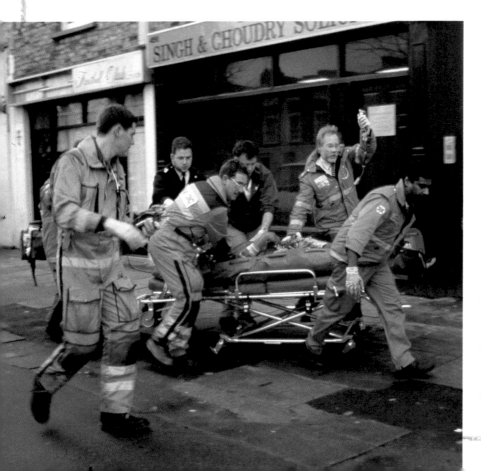

◀ Doctors, emergency workers, and paramedics who attend accidents are all trained to do artificial resuscitation.

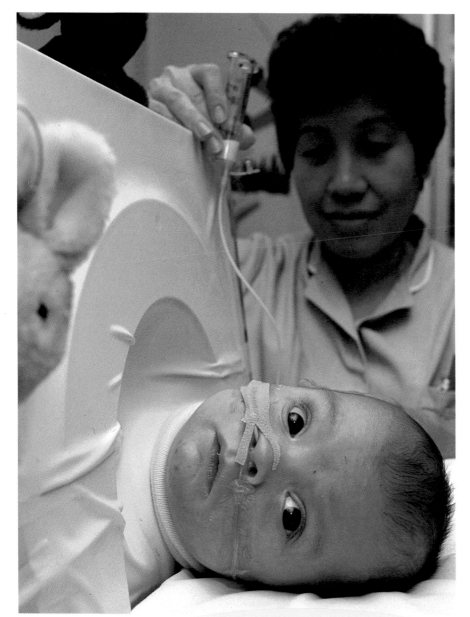

◄ This little boy has paralyzed breathing muscles. An iron lung machine is helping him to breathe.

Did you know?

Some diseases, such as polio, may stop the muscles used for breathing from working. This means the person with the disease could die from suffocation. The first life-saving iron lung was designed in 1929. In an iron lung a pump creates a vacuum in an airtight box that encloses the patient's chest. The pump works in such a way that the vacuum is on and then off. Each time the vacuum is on, the pressure of the air is greater outside the box than inside both it and the patient's chest. So air is sucked into the patient's chest.

Glossary

Addictive Makes you crave for more, or want more.

Air sacs Thin-walled endings to the breathing tubes. This is where oxygen from the air you breathe in is transferred into your blood.

Allergens Substances that produce a reaction in the body and prevent it working properly.

Alveoli See **Air sacs**.

Artificial resuscitation Act of reviving a person who has stopped breathing.

Asphyxia Being unable to breathe.

Asthma Condition that affects the breathing tubes and makes it hard to breathe.

Breathing organ Structure in animals where oxygen passes into the blood.

Breathing system Tubes and structures in the body that allow you to breathe.

Bronchi Two tubes which branch from the windpipe and lead to the lungs.

Bronchioles Fine tubes inside the lungs that transport air to the air sacs.

Bronchitis Disease of the bronchi and bronchioles.

Capillary Very fine blood vessel.

Carbon dioxide One of the gases in the air. It is also the waste gas given off by cells when they use oxygen to burn food to release energy. Blood collects it from the cells, carries it to the lungs, and it is breathed out.

Carbon monoxide Gas found in car exhaust fumes.

Cartilage Firm smooth substance.

Catalytic converter Device fitted to car exhausts, which reduces the amount of dangerous gases in exhaust fumes.

Cells Tiny 'building blocks' of living things.

Cilia Tiny hairs on the surface of cells. The hairs beat in a rythmical way.

De-oxygenated blood Dull red blood that is poor in oxygen, rich in carbon dioxide.

Diaphragm Sheet of tissue in your body that separates the chest from the lower body.

Epileptic Seizure which people who suffer from epilepsy, a nervous disease, may have.

Esophagus Muscular tube between the throat and the stomach that aids in digestion.

Exhale Breathe out.

Frequency Number of vibrations per second produced in the vocal chords during speech.

Gills Organ in fish for obtaining oxygen from water.

House dust mite Tiny spider-like animals found in house dust. They are too small for you to see them.

Inhaler Device used by asthma sufferers to spray helpful drugs into their lungs.

Inhale Breathe in.

Intonation Changes in the pitch of a voice speaking.

Language Combination of sounds into the words that are used to communicate between people.

Larynx Part of the windpipe containing the vocal cords.

Mucus Slimy substance made by cells.

Nasal cavity Spaces in the head that are linked to the nostrils.

Nicotine Poisonous chemical that is the chief ingredient of tobacco.

Nitrogen Gas that makes up 80% of the air.

Oxygen Gas in air which is used in the body to release energy from food.

Oxygenated blood Bright red blood, which is rich in oxygen.

Passive smoking Breathing in air that contains other people's cigarette smoke.

Pitch Your voice is high- or low-pitched depending on the frequency of vibration of your vocal cord.

Pleura Layers of tissue between the lungs and ribs, which help to make breathing movements smooth.

Pollen Fine powder made by flowering plants.

Pollution Damage to the surroundings caused by human activities, especially by waste products.

Red blood cells Cells in the blood which carry oxygen.

Respiration Process in living cells which releases energy from food.

Rib cage Protective structure inside your chest. It is formed by your ribs, bones which protect your heart and lungs, and which help to bring about breathing movements.

Sinuses Spaces in the bones at the front of the skull.

Soft palate Found at the back of the roof of the mouth.

Speech Sounds formed into words.

Suffocation Condition in which a person is deprived of oxygen.

Sulphur dioxide Waste gas found in some factory smoke.

Tar Substance breathed in with cigarette smoke.

Trachea Windpipe that leads from your mouth to your chest.

Uvula Projection at the back of the soft palate.

Vocal cords Two membranes (thin sheets of tissue) stretched across the space inside the voice box.

Voice box See **Larynx.**

Water vapor Water in gas form.

Windpipe See **Trachea.**

Womb Part of a woman's body where a fertilized egg develops into a baby.

Index

Further Reading

Bryan, Jenny. *Breathing: The Respiratory System.* Morristown, N.J.: Dillon, 1993.

Parker, Steve. 1992. *Catching a Cold: How You Get Ill, Suffer and Recover.* Danbury, Ct.: Franklin Watts, 1992.

Suzuki, David. *Looking At the Body.* New York: Wiley, 1991.